BIBLE VISUALS international

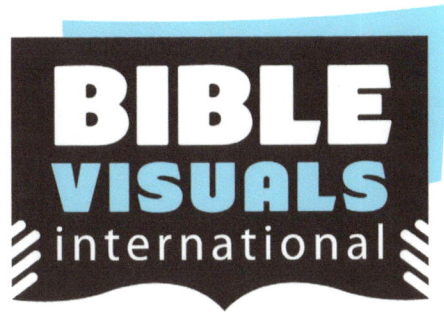

Helping Children See Jesus

ISBN: 978-1-64104-102-7

Doctor in the Pygmy Forest

Author: Lois Headley Dick
Artist: Vernon Henkel   Computer Graphic Artist: Yuko Willoughby
Page Layout: Patricia Pope, Charity Taft

© 2020 Bible Visuals International
PO Box 153, Akron, PA 17501-0153
Phone: (717) 859-1131
www.biblevisuals.org

RELATED ITEMS

To access related items (such as activities, memory verse posters and translated texts) please visit our web store at shop.biblevisuals.org and enter 5095 in the search box on the page.

FREE TEXT DOWNLOAD

To access a FREE printable copy of the teaching text (PDF format) in English or other available languages, enter S5095DL in the search box. Add the item to your cart, and use coupon code XTACSV17 at checkout. Once your order is processed you will receive an email with a link to the free download.

STUDENT ACTIVITES

These are included with the FREE printable copy of the English teaching text for this story. See the directions under Free Text Download (above) to access them.

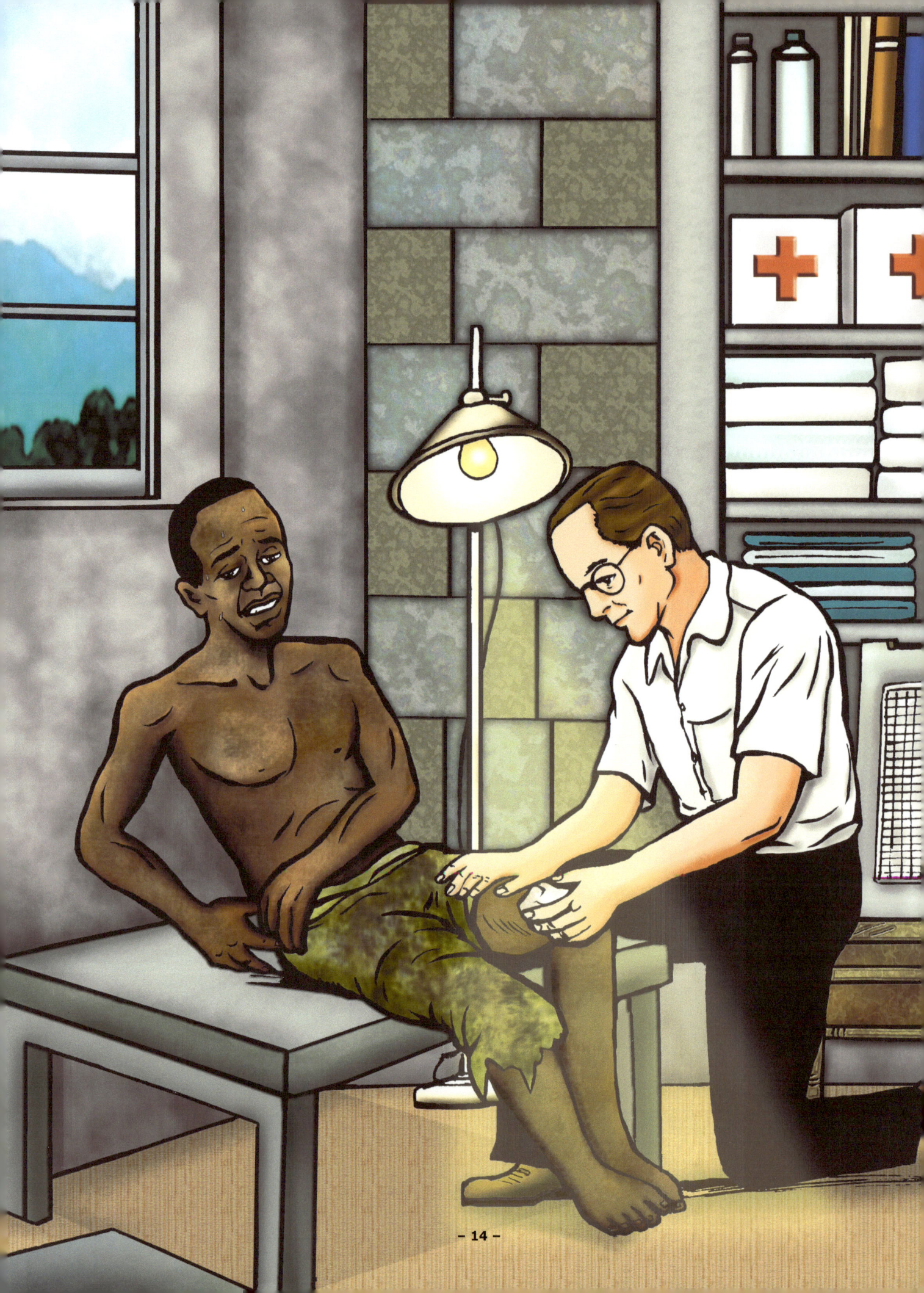

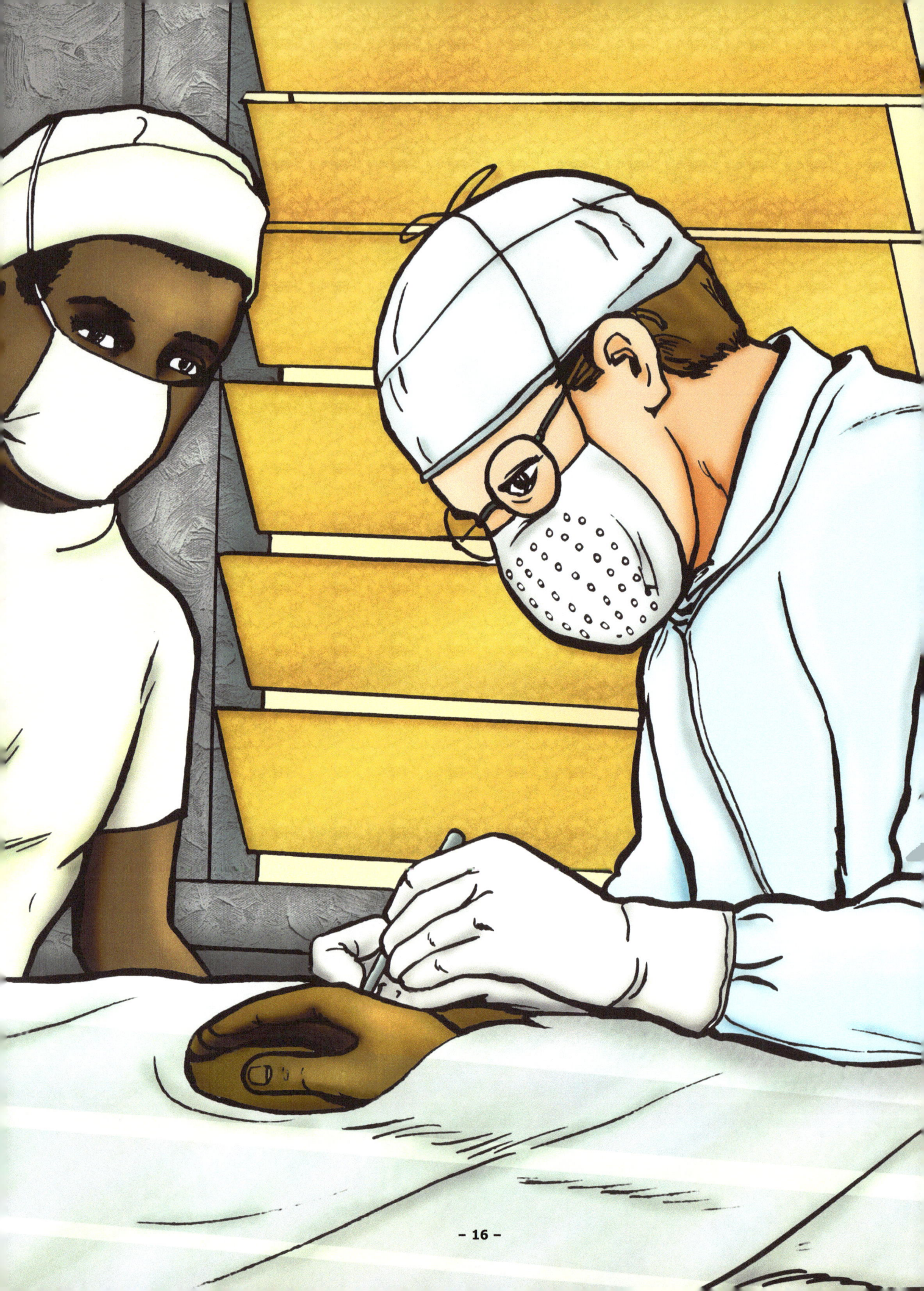

ELECTRIC
LIGHT
FIXTURES

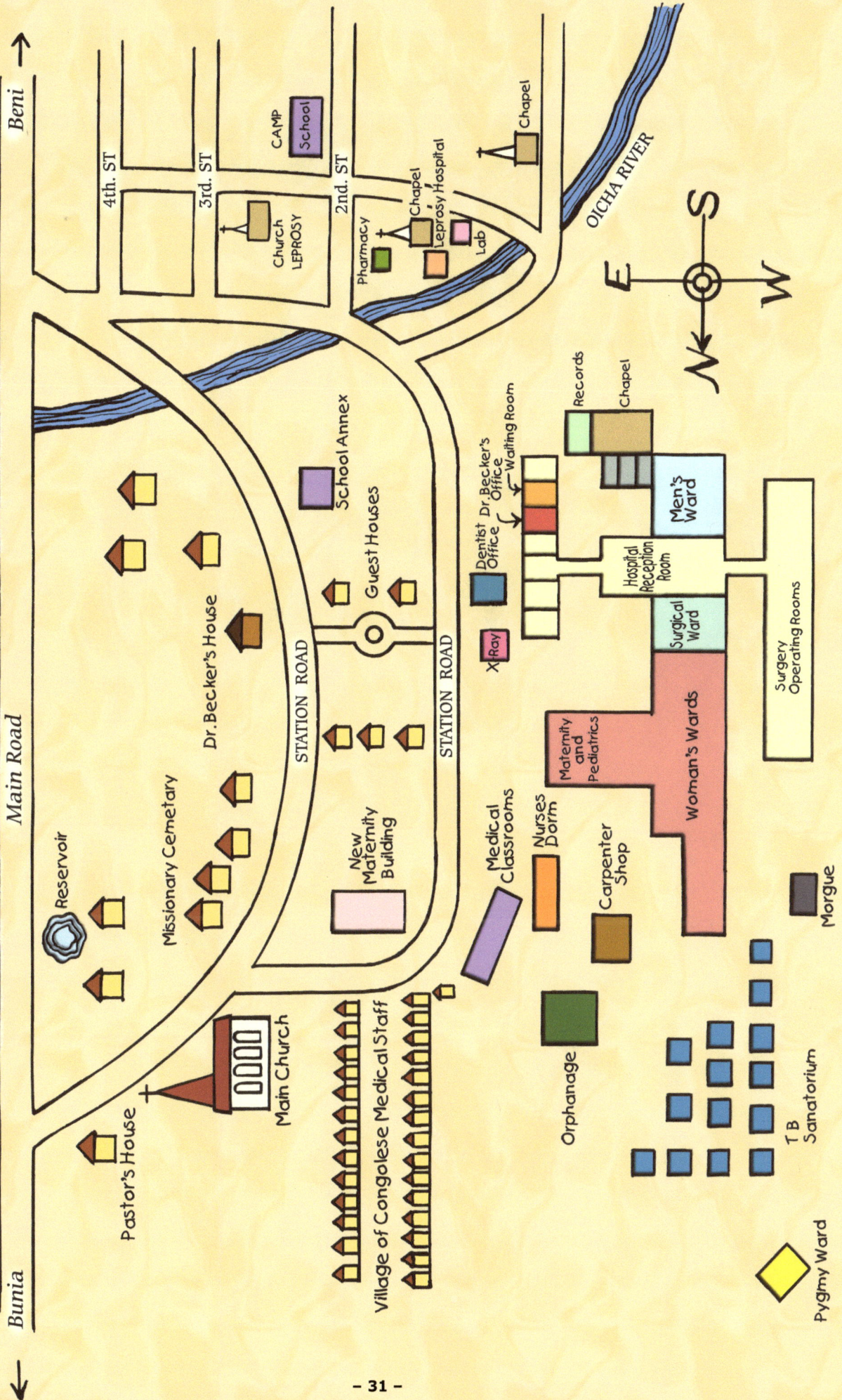

MAP OF OICHA

Bunia ← Main Road → Beni

Pastor's House

Reservoir

Missionary Cemetery

Dr. Becker's House

Main Church

Village of Congolese Medical Staff

New Maternity Building

STATION ROAD

School Annex

Guest Houses

STATION ROAD

Medical Classrooms

Nurses Dorm

Carpenter Shop

Orphanage

Woman's Wards

Maternity and Pediatrics

Surgical Ward

Surgery Operating Rooms

Men's Ward

Hospital Reception Room

Dr. Becker's Office

Waiting Room

Records

Chapel

Dentist

X-Ray

Morgue

T B Sanatorium

Pygmy Ward

4th. ST

3rd. ST

2nd. ST

CAMP

School

Church LEPROSY

Pharmacy

Chapel

Leprosy Hospital

Lab

Chapel

OICHA RIVER

E — N — W

S

FRENCH CONGO

SUDAN

Congo River

Bunia

Oicha

Ruwenzori

Nyabirongo

Kitsombiro

Equator

UGANDA

Lake Victoria

Lake Tanganyika

BELGIUM CONGO (ZAIRE)

Leopoldville

Position of main map

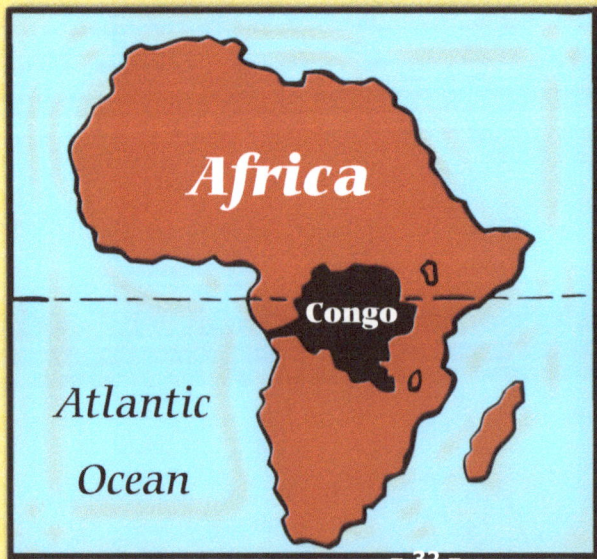

Africa

Congo

Atlantic Ocean

And the prayer of faith shall save the sick, and the Lord shall raise him up; and if he have committed sins, they shall be forgiven him.

James 5:15

Chapter 1

CURSED BY THE WITCH DOCTOR

. . . Ye turned to God from idols to serve the living and true God.
(1 Thessalonians 1:9b)

NOTE TO THE TEACHER

Display each illustration where indicated in text, laying volume aside when the story line continues beyond the picture. Show the map of the Congo on the back cover. Briefly discuss facts about Africa, the Congo and a jungle. You may want to read the historical details at the end of Chapter 5 to give you a sense of the timing of this story.

The extra activities on pages 14 are correlated with each chapter and encourage student involvement. A master for memory verse tokens is located on page 15.

We are grateful for the help of the following missionary nurses who worked with Dr. Becker and provided photographs and slides for illustrating this story: Miss Virginia Landis, Miss Olive I. Rawn, Mrs. Vera (Thiessen) Hillis

Pronunciation Guide

Aba	Ah' - bah	Munganga	Mun - gahn' - gah
Abu	Ah' - boo	Nyabirongo	Knee - ah - beer - ohn' - go
Babira	Bah - beer' - ah		
Ituri	Ee - tour' - ee	Nyankunde	Knee - ahn - kun' - dee
Kisobe	Key - so' - beh		
Kitsombiro	Keet - sour - beer' - oh	Oicha	O - wee' - cha
Kivu	Key' - voo	Swahili	Swa - he' - lee
Lingala	Ling - gal' - ah	Vubisi	Voo - bee' - see
Miseberi	Me - suh - berry'	Wanandi	Wah - nahn' - dee
Munandi	Moo - nahn' - dee		

Show Illustration #1

Early one morning, Dr. Carl Becker, a medical missionary, left his mud hut and almost stepped on a long piece of hollow bamboo lying on the path directly in front of his home. The bamboo was covered with egg yolk and had a bit of leopard skin dangling out. Dr. Becker picked up the strange object and sniffed. Castor oil! Walking to the end of the hut, he showed the bamboo to another missionary, Paul Hurlburt.

"The witch doctor did it," said Mr. Hurlburt. "It's a hex, a native curse."

"But why?"

"He wants to get rid of you. Now the people will watch you. If you cough, they will say the curse made you sick. If one of your patients dies, they'll blame you. He hopes to frighten you away."

Dr. Becker looked past the grass-roofed mud huts and over the hillsides in the distance. There were over 100 villages in the area and many of the Africans were suspicious of the missionary doctor. *I must win their trust*, Dr. Becker thought as he turned to Paul.

"What kind of illnesses do the Africans have?" he asked.

"Around here it's mostly pneumonia, flu, bronchitis as well as some malaria, dysentery and leprosy," Paul answered. "But don't expect the sick to flock to you for help. They always go to the witch doctors first. The witch doctors rule the people by fear. They say evil spirits and demons cause illness. The people must bring presents to the witch doctors to pay for the hexes or spells to keep away illness and accident. Your treatment of your first patient is very important."

The treatment of any patient is important, thought Dr. Becker as he headed toward his hut.

In 1929, the doctor and his wife, Marie, with their two children, arrived in the heart of Africa. They had traveled 12,000 miles from Pennsylvania to the Belgian Congo. Their first home at Kitsombiro had two rooms made of mud still soft and wet when they arrived. There, 8,000 feet up in the mountains of eastern Congo, Dr. Becker was the only doctor for miles around.

Show Illustration #2

One day Dr. Becker found an African woman with a painful hernia crouched outside his door. (A hernia is a large bulge which must be repaired by a surgeon quickly so the blood supply is not cut off.) She had already been to three witch doctors. They used their medicines along with chanting, dancing and spells, but the woman became worse. Now she was in great pain.

With his wife and Paul Hurlburt helping, Dr. Becker placed the patient on the kitchen table and operated. Twelve unfriendly warriors surrounded the hut. If the woman lived, they would spread the word and everybody would want to try the foreign doctor's medicine.

But what if she died! Dr. Becker thought of the bamboo hex on his path. Before the operation he closed his eyes and prayed.

God answered prayer! The operation was a success. In a few days the woman returned to her village and told everyone of the kind foreign doctor.

Now village drums throbbed out an exciting message: "Come to Kitsombiro! The *munganga* is wiser than the witch doctors." While the drums beat, witch doctors sulked and plotted revenge. But people began to arrive from the surrounding villages.

Though Dr. Becker served at six other villages, eventually most of his work was at Oicha. This small village clearing in Kivu Province, was deep in the Ituri Forest where the pygmies lived. Mission work at Oicha had been begun to reach these little people, but they seemed afraid to come out of the forest for medical help. The other African tribes around Oicha didn't think pygmies were human and treated them unkindly, so the pygmies remained by themselves in the woods.

Show Illustration #3

A chief named Kisobe ruled Oicha. He was afraid of no one. He respected no one. He loved no one except his little son Benjamina.

In 1929, before Dr. Becker had come to Oicha, a missionary named Jim Bell had visited Kisobe to ask permission to clear land and build a mission station. "We will build a church where you can learn about the one true God," he had said.

Kisobe shook his head. "I have my own gods."

"We will even build a small hospital. If you are ever sick or hurt, you can stay there and be made well."

Chief Kisobe swung his head stubbornly from side to side. "I have my own personal witch doctor. He can scare away the worst demons."

"We will build a school," Jim went on. "Your little boy will learn to read."

Kisobe's eyes rolled up in his head and a smile showed strong, white teeth. He had heard of reading, where a piece of paper told wonderful stories. He wanted his son to have everything. "Build your mission station," he said.

Other missionaries helped Jim Bell chop down trees and build log cabins, a chapel, a medical clinic and a school. Then came the day when Benjamina ran to his father and showed him black scribbling in a book. "This is God's Book," said the boy. "It says, `Do not murder. Do not get drunk. Do not cheat people'."

Kisobe scowled. He didn't intend to change his way of life. He liked to dance all night and get drunk on banana beer. He reportedly killed, cooked and ate his enemies. If twin babies were born in his village, he ordered one killed to remove the awful curse. Was he supposed to give up all of that?

He noticed that his own people attended the small chapel, sang and smiled more. They said they had received the Lord Yesu (Jesus) as their Saviour from sin.

Show Illustration #4

Kisobe went off into the bush to visit his witch doctor and talk it over. "The foreign missionary says the blood of this Yesu takes away sin."

"The blood of a chicken is enough," the witch doctor replied.

"The missionary says Yesu forgives free without asking payment." He eyed his friend shrewdly.

"I ask only a goat sometimes. And I don't ask you to change your way of living, do I?"

Kisobe heaved a sigh and returned home. He wanted to forget Yesu, but even his own children sang about Him.

Years went by, and then Dr. Becker moved to Oicha. Once again the drums spread the news: "Come to Oicha! The foreign doctor heals many people!" Sick and injured people who lived far away traveled the jungle paths from Kenya, Uganda and other places outside the Congo. They came by the hundreds.

Most shocking of all to Kisobe, Benjamina announced that he believed in Yesu and wanted to become a doctor!

The people of Oicha loved Dr. Becker. Every day they began lining up before dawn, hundreds of them. Dr. Becker could see only the worst cases. Three afternoons a week he operated.

Usually he performed about 24 surgeries a week, but there were also emergencies.

An important part of Dr. Becker's day was his prayer time and Bible reading from 5:00 to 6:00 a.m. Later, after breakfast, he and his wife read the Bible and prayed together. In the beginning, they also studied Swahili and Lingala. (Swahili was the trade language of the Congo and Lingala was the trade language of the Congo River.) One day they talked about changes since they had arrived in Africa.

"Do you remember Abu?" asked the doctor. "I gave him a bottle of medicine. I told him to take one swallow when the sun is high overhead. Then another swallow before he sleeps. I didn't see him for two weeks. Finally I visited his village."

"Yes," interrupted Mrs. Becker. "There was the bottle of medicine dangling from a string tied to the roof. He hung it there to scare away the evil spirits. He didn't understand, and he felt much worse. I also remember when you gave another man six pills. 'Take one a day,' you said."

"Oh, yes. He pasted them all around his waist as good luck charms!"

Now the doctor made sure his patients took their medicine while someone watched them. He trained African helpers to be his assistants, including Benjamina.

Show Illustration #5

As Dr. Becker and his wife spoke, they heard shouting. Down the dirt road to the clinic, came four men carrying Chief Kisobe on a grass mat. He was moaning and holding his belly. Benjamina explained: "My father has a large, painful hernia. I told him you could easily fix it, but he went to the witch doctor instead."

"I gave the witch doctor one of my fattest chickens!" wailed Chief Kisobe. "He put on his feathered hat and danced around me for hours. He put bad-smelling stuff on the hernia. He made me worse! Oh, the pain!"

"We'll operate right away," Dr. Becker said. "I'm afraid you waited too long, but we will also pray for you. Lift him to the table," he told his helpers.

The doctor washed the chief's belly and cleansed it with Iodine. A missionary nurse and Benjamina scrubbed their hands and put on rubber gloves to assist. "Lord, guide these hands to do Your will. In Jesus' name, amen," prayed Dr. Becker.

There was one more thing the doctor had to say, "Chief, we will do our best. If you should die, what will you say to God when you see Him? You have refused His way of salvation. Will you repent now and receive Jesus as your Saviour?"

Kisobe was frightened and in great pain. He was afraid to die. So he nodded his head–yes!

The nurse gave him anesthesia so he slept soundly. Then the doctor operated swiftly. Everything seemed fine. But because the chief was very old, his heart stopped beating. "My father is dead!" cried Benjamina.

Quickly Dr. Becker gave medicine to start the heart beating again. In a while Chief Kisobe woke up quite dizzy, looked around and said, "Why are you just standing there doing nothing? Fix my hernia so I can go back home!"

The doctor laughed. "You're all fixed."

Kisobe's body was mended, but he had only pretended to receive Christ because he had been afraid. His life didn't change. He drove Benjamina–his own son–out of his village because he was a Christian. He ordered his people to stop going to Dr. Becker. "Go only to the witch doctor," he commanded.

Kisobe hardened his heart, and his life became even more sinful.

Show Illustration #6

One time after dark another witch doctor visited Dr. Becker secretly. "Greetings, munganga," he began. "You have been stealing away the hearts of my patients. Now I come to ask your advice. I have a sickness. I have not been able to enchant it away."

Dr. Becker sat down with him and answered all his questions about medicine. He noticed that the man had a large hernia which caused him much pain. The witch doctor would not agree to an operation. He shook his head at the doctor's explanations. "No, no! Evil spirits make the sickness."

Finally he rose to go, but the doctor could not let him leave without telling him again of God who loved him enough to send His Son Jesus to die for his sin.

The witch doctor went back to his hut trusting instead in snake skins, bird feathers, leopard's teeth and claws, cowrie shells, and hollow gourds with rattling pebbles inside. Most of all, he trusted and feared evil spirits. He never became a Christian.

But the witch doctor thought about Dr. Becker's talk. Little by little, he stopped scaring people away from the doctor. Finally he began to call him, "my friend, the white witch doctor."

Later other witch doctors brought all their spells and hexes and magic equipment and burned them in public. They had received Christ as Saviour and had renounced Satan and his worship.

Chief Kisobe watched all this in silence.

Show Illustration #7

Chief Kisobe wasn't getting any younger. His body was wearing out. He had aches, pains and poor eyesight. He lost weight and limped as he walked. And he was afraid all the time! He was afraid of evil spirits, curses and spells from a witch doctor.

The Bible says, "There is no peace, saith my God, to the wicked" (Isaiah 57:21). Chief Kisobe sat outside his hut remembering all the bad things

he had done. Spilling the blood of chickens and goats had not given him peace. Now he had another fear that was heavy on his heart. Just before his operation he had lied to Dr. Becker's God, the greatest God of all. What if God struck him dead for lying?

Time passed. Kisobe watched Oicha grow larger and spread out like a small city. Trees were cut down to let sunshine in and keep the leopards away.

One Sunday he sat outside his hut and watched hundreds of people from neighboring villages hurry past toward Oicha. Soon a car stopped and his old friend, missionary Jim Bell, greeted him.

"Chief, we're all going to Oicha to hear a preacher from America. Come with us and give your heart to God now. You're not ready to die and you know it!"

Kisobe thought it over silently. *Maybe this is my last chance. Death will come soon. God has been very patient.*

"I have trouble walking," he said. "Will you take me in the car?"

"Of course."

Show Illustration #8

Driving, it wasn't far to Oicha and they pulled up to the large orange-brick church. "Please park under the open window," said Kisobe. "If I go in, the people will stare and point or laugh."

After the Bible message, the preacher said, "if you want to accept the Lord Jesus Christ as Saviour, come to the front of the chapel." With great difficulty the Chief got out of the car. "I want to go in the church and walk up front and be saved. I really mean it this time."

Everyone was startled and happy to see Kisobe accept Christ as his Saviour. All the Chief's sins were forgiven and forgotten because of Jesus.

Kisobe was soon too weak and sick to attend church every Sunday. He was disappointed. He wanted everyone to know he was a Christian and had a new life.

One day he said, "*Munganga*, I see you are building more rooms on to the hospital. I, too, am going to build something. I am going to build a chapel in my village."

And it was done. The power of the witch doctor over Chief Kisobe was broken. The power of God was greater. Through medicine and Dr. Becker's treatment, people, including witch doctors, came to know the one true God.

Chapter 2
HOW DO YOU MAKE A DOCTOR?
I will instruct thee and teach thee in the way which thou shalt go: I will guide thee with mine eye.
(Psalm 32:8)

Carl K. Becker was born on January 30, 1894 in Manheim, PA. As a small boy he attended Sunday School at a Reformed Church in the morning, then walked two miles with his father, brother Frank and sister Helen to attend afternoon Sunday services in a village called Sporting Hill.

When Carl was 11 years old, his father died. His mother worked in a factory to earn money to buy food and clothing. Carl, already in ninth grade, was getting better grades than the older boys. He was also becoming interested in medicine.

One day after catechism class,* the pastor of the Reformed

Church said to him, "Carl, you have to make a personal decision for Christ. Even though your parents are Christians, you must come to God yourself. The Lord Jesus died in your place. He shed His blood so you could be forgiven of your sin."

That day Carl accepted Christ. His life changed. Now he didn't do everything his friends did. Instead, he began to pray and read more of the Bible every night. He wanted to obey God.

*Catechism class teaches young people what their church believes about God and the Bible.

Show Illustration #9

Carl's Sunday School teacher was Mrs. Anna Kraedy. The boys in her class loved her, and because of Mrs. Kraedy's love for God's Word, they learned to love His Word too.

Mrs. Kraedy was also concerned about missions. She told her class that deep in the middle of Africa there were millions of people who had never heard the Gospel. "The Belgian Congo," she said, "is full of cannibals, lions and giant snakes. It's not safe at all! But Africa Inland Mission wants to send missionaries there."

The Belgian Congo! These were mysterious, shivery words Carl remembered from history class. Something stirred in his heart. *Could I go there*? he wondered.

A little later, Mr. Lee Downing of Africa Inland Mission spent three weeks in Manheim and Carl talked to him about medical missions.

"Why do you need missionary doctors?" Carl asked. "I thought missionaries just preached and taught the Bible."

"Doctors prepare the way for preachers and teachers, Carl. The Africans live in fear of disease which they think is a curse from evil spirits. The witch doctor uses that fear. He makes the people bring him many gifts without helping them. A missionary can't just preach to somebody who has a toothache, or who is bleeding or choking or hurting. He must also care for the needs of the body."

Carl thought about that for many days. Was God calling him to be a missionary doctor? He would love to be a doctor. But it would take six years to go through medical school.

One night he fell to his knees on a grass plot behind their small house and prayed, "Lord, if You will help me become a doctor, I will be a missionary if You call me."

Carl was only 15 when he graduated from high school. The following year he went to Mercersburg Academy, then Ursinus College. But after a year there, he left and worked at various jobs to support his mother. When he was 22, Carl entered Hahnemann Medical College in Philadelphia with only $125.

Show Illustration #10

Life became all study and hard work. By the end of his first year, Carl worked at two jobs. Nights he served ice cream and made sodas at a soda fountain in the Reading Terminal train station. A few hours a day he worked in a deli.

After classes, Carl returned to the third floor apartment he shared with three other students. He lived in his only worn-out suit and a pair of broken-down shoes. In spite of his jobs, money was running out.

Then World War I began during Carl's second year in medical school. America entered the war and Carl joined a reserve medical corps. The corps moved its members into the local armory. Carl found, to his surprise, that now he had free room and board, a uniform to wear, plus thirty dollars a month! God was taking care of him.

Finally in 1921 after five years in school, Carl was ready to graduate. One day a month before graduation, he prayed, "Lord, all I have that is fit to wear are my army shoes and the old coat. My mother and sister will be embarrassed when they see me. Will you help me?"

Within a week, Carl received $100 in checks from friends. His simple faith in his heavenly Father would help him later in the Congo.

Show Illustration #11 (left side)

During college Carl had sometimes visited his mother in Reading, PA. On one visit, his brother Frank introduced him to a young school teacher, Marie Bodey. She was a Christian. One of the first things Carl told her was, "Marie, my life belongs to God. I don't know where He'll send me. I promised Him that if He helped me become a doctor, I would go anywhere He asks."

Marie agreed absolutely that God and His will should always come first in their lives. During the following months Carl and Marie grew to love each other.

Show Illustration #11 (right side)

At Hahnemann, the rules stated that new doctors must work for their hospital a year. During that year Carl met Charles Hurlburt of Africa Inland Mission, who had lived for many years in Africa. (*Teacher*: Charles Hurlburt is the father of Paul Hurlburt, who was mentioned in Chapter 1.)

"Carl, we need missionary doctors. We've discovered a tribe of two hundred thousand people called Babira. The witch doctors with their native 'medicine' have caused the death of more people than the slave traders. We can't send just a preacher in there. We need. . . ."

". . . a doctor." Carl finished the sentence for him.

"We don't have a doctor to send."

Is God calling me to Africa? Carl wondered. But his mother was a widow. And Carl remembered a verse he had read in the Bible: "If any man provide not for his own, and especially for those of his own house, he hath denied the faith, and is worse than an infidel" (1 Timothy 5:8). Carl knew that meant his first duty was to care for his mother.

In 1922 Dr. Carl Becker moved to Boyertown, PA. He was 28 years old. The three doctors who had taken care of the townspeople had moved away. Dr. Becker found plenty of patients waiting for him. Three months later he married Marie Bodey.

Show Illustration #12

In those days, doctors made house calls, visiting people at home who were too sick or injured to go to a hospital. One night, in the middle of a snow storm, two farmers woke Carl by hammering on the door. Dr. Becker grabbed his black bag and hurried outside. One farmer called above the howl of the wind, "We have no electricity out our way because of the storm!"

Dr. Becker hurried to his next-door neighbor, Dr. Bornemann. "You'll have to assist me tonight," he said to the dentist, as they climbed into the doctor's car. At the farmhouse, by the light of a flashlight, Dr. Becker brought a baby safely into the world.

Seven years passed in Boyertown. Dr. Becker still hadn't kept his promise to God, although he and Marie prayed about missions. God hadn't shown Dr. Becker yet how He wanted him to serve. Instead, God allowed Dr. Becker to put money into the bank for his mother.

During this time three important events occurred:

1. Dr. Becker was asked by a government official to move to Washington, D.C., where he could make more money as a doctor.
2. A wealthy man in Boyertown offered to build him a big, new hospital if he stayed there. Then Boyertown would grow, and the doctor would earn more money.
3. A letter came from Mr. Charles Hurlburt of AIM saying their missionary doctor had died of blackwater fever because there was no one to care for her. There was no mention of money.

The need in Africa for doctors–especially in the Congo–was greater than ever. But Dr. Becker was earning $10,000 a year, a lot of money at the time!

One evening as the doctor was in his office praying, the Holy Spirit, who lives within every Christian, spoke to his heart. It was that simple. Dr. Becker called Marie into the room.

"My dear, do you remember my promise to God that I made 10 years ago? Tonight God definitely reminded me of it. I think He wants us to be missionaries. I'm going to write Mr. Hurlburt."

Three letters came flying back from Mr. Hurlburt, one after another. He was thrilled to know Dr. Becker would go to the Congo. "How soon can you be ready?" he wrote.

Show Illustration #13

Mrs. Becker, six-year-old Mary and three-year-old Carl were happy about the decision. Soon the news spread all over Boyertown. But the people weren't happy. "We don't want to lose our doctor!" they exclaimed.

Local businessmen announced a meeting at the American Legion building, a rally in honor of the doctor. He was embarrassed at seeing four hundred people applaud and cheer him and beg him to stay in Boyertown.

What he said to them was simple and direct. "Many years ago I made a promise to God that I would give my life for His use if He would help me become a doctor. I am going to the Belgian Congo."

Dr. Becker was promised $60 a month while on the mission field. He was earning 14 times that much in Boyertown. However, the same God who had provided new clothes for his graduation from medical school would take care of him and his family.

In August 1929 they left home taking their car and many 60-pound bundles of medical equipment and belongings.

In October, after crossing the Atlantic Ocean by ship and crossing Europe by train, they traveled across the Mediterranean Sea, through Egypt, then farther south until they reached the Congo. Finally, after a 25 mile hike up the side of a mountain, the family reached Kitsombiro and their first home–a mud hut.

Show Illustration #14

Paul Hurlburt welcomed the Beckers. "You'll have to share our hut until we build one for you," he said motioning to his two-room home. "It will be crowded since we have five children. But you can have one room. We just added it for you." Turning to Mrs. Becker he continued, "We don't cook indoors. I'm afraid you'll have to learn to cook over those three stones behind the hut. And, after you're settled, Dr. Becker, you'll need to get acquainted with your future patients." He pointed to some tribesmen standing among the trees in the distance.

Show Illustration #1

It was several days later when Dr. Becker stepped outside and found the witch doctor's curse.

Dr. Becker stepped out of his car. It was good to be back at Aba where Marie waited in their home. Home had been many places this first term. First Kitsombiro, then Miseberi, and for a while, Aba. And now they were to move again.

> **NOTE TO THE TEACHER**
>
> Dr. Becker assumed he was sailing to Africa in 1929 under AIM. He didn't know that Charles Hurlburt had resigned from AIM because of ill health, then 2 years later founded the Unevangelized Africa Mission. His son, Paul Hurlburt, was the head of the mission. In 1928 UAM sent 10 missionaries to the Congo. So, actually, Dr. Becker first entered Africa under UAM. In 1931, he applied to AIM and was accepted.

Show Illustration #11 (left half)

"Jim Bell wants us to help in the medical clinic at Oicha, Marie. He wants to spend more time trying to reach the pygmies," Dr. Becker said later. "The Field Council has assigned us there." He paused. "I learned some other news. The folks at home who were sending the $60 a month for our support have had financial difficulties. It sounds like they won't be able to support us."

"But God has always met our needs, Carl," Marie responded.

"And He will continue to do the same as we continue to serve Him," her husband said confidently.

The Beckers settled into their leaf-roofed home at Oicha. The mission station at Oicha had been cut out of the jungle. Tall trees had been chopped down to let in sunlight. Ground had been cleared and mud huts built. Now that Dr. Becker spent more time at Oicha, more people came to the dispensary. Soon a row of ten mud huts were added for patients. Then, on the other side of a banana grove, three small huts were built for leprosy patients. And still the people came, but no pygmies.

One day Dr. Becker announced he was starting a school to train assistants to help him.

"What?" friends cried. "Take a jungle boy who is used to more play than work, who probably attended a mission school only to third grade, a boy with no feeling of responsibility or sense of time, and let him assist a doctor?"

But Dr. Becker had faith in a great God. The boys he trained learned to treat common diseases. They passed the exams from the Belgian Colonial Government and returned to Oicha to care for almost half of the patients. Dr. Becker was able to perform more operations and care for serious cases.

The doctor was also a friend to his helpers. He taught them in a Bible class, told them about world events, and invited them to his home. He lived before them as a Christian should live.

One day a poor, pitiful man named Lazaro was brought to Oicha dying of gangrene and ulcers. He was from a primitive tribe the other Africans looked down upon.

Show Illustration #15

"He needs a blood transfusion," said Dr. Becker. "One of the medical students will have the honor of giving blood to Lazaro. Nurse, please take blood samples."

The students ran away and hid. No one wanted to give blood to this low tribesman. The doctor insisted upon the blood samples. Only one student had the same blood type as Lazaro.

"Will you save Lazaro's life?" the doctor asked him.

"No! No! I will give my blood for anyone else–but not for him!"

The doctor rolled up his own sleeve. "All right, I will give my blood to Lazaro. I'm the same blood type. Will you please take a pint of my blood?"

The student couldn't believe he heard correctly. The foreign doctor was willing to give his blood to the patient who lay on the stretcher. Shame swept over him.

"Doctor, take my blood. I'll do it! You are not even of the African race, yet you are willing to give your blood. And Jesus, God's Son, gave His blood for me and He was divine!"

Afterward, Dr. Becker showed the students a verse in the Bible: "He hath made of one blood all nations of men to dwell on all the face of the earth" (Acts 17:26).

There is no such thing as American blood, African blood, tribal blood, royal blood, French blood, German blood, or any other national difference of human blood.

Within two years 300 patients a day came to the clinic. Dr. Becker was doing one thousand operations a year. There were also 175 leprosy patients now. A hospital was needed. But Dr. Becker would not ask anyone for money. He would not even mention his needs to anyone. He said to his staff, "God said He would supply our needs. Let's just trust Him." And they did.

Money came little by little. A small hospital was started. The dispensary was enlarged. Houses were built for patients. A small village for tuberculosis patients was developed. Oicha was growing.

Dr. Becker kept his operating room clean and sterile even though he was in the middle of a jungle. Instruments were washed and sterilized. Doctor and nurses washed their hands often and wore surgical gloves for operations.

At the end of one long, busy day, two medical aides carried an old man from the forest into the hospital. He was barely alive and was covered with mud. He smelled of filth. The medics laid him down and quickly turned away.

Alice, one of the African nurses, had just finished cleaning the operating room. She ran to get Dr. Becker.

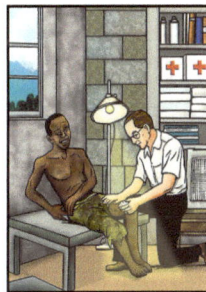

Show Illustration #16

"Another serious hernia," pronounced the doctor. "Get the operating room ready, please."

"For that dirty old man?" Alice exclaimed.

"Every person is precious in the sight of the Lord," replied Dr. Becker.

"Even this miserable creature?" Alice persisted.

"Everyone," repeated the doctor firmly. He operated upon him just as carefully and prayerfully as though the man had been a chief or government official.

Alice and the medics never forgot the doctor's words: "Every person is precious."

At the time Dr. Becker was in the Congo, 40 percent of the African people had leprosy. Leprosy was considered incurable and highly contagious, but research proved this to be incorrect.

Leprosy is a disease where patches of skin lose their color and ability to feel anything: heat, cold, sharp, dull, soft, hard. The patches, or lumps, develop on the ears, nose, or even all over the body. A leprosy patient can be easily hurt if he touches something scalding hot or if he steps on a sharp object. Many leprosy patients become deformed and disabled from complications.

Show Illustration #17

The leprosy patients at Oicha lived near the hospital in huts of sun-dried brick. Each patient was given one-half acre of land to grow vegetables. Every week they received injections of chaulmoogra oil. This restored the pigment, but did not cure the disease. The new medicine in the form of pills, a sulfa drug, came and the treatment brought such good results that more leprosy patients arrived. Soon the forest had to be cleared to enlarge the village. Eventually 4,000 patients plus their families lived at Oicha.

In 1954, Dr. Becker had a famous visitor at Oicha. Dr. Robert Cochrane was the world's authority on leprosy. He had visited mission stations all over the world. The leprosy village at Oicha was the largest in Africa, second largest in the world. Dr. Cochrane praised the work at Oicha.

Show Illustration #18

Dr. Becker had learned to operate on leprosy patients. His first surgery was on a hand so the twisted fingers could straighten out and be useful again. Then the patient would exercise the hand every day for weeks.

The fingers on Munandi's hand had twisted into a claw. He was sure he could never use his hands again. Once Munandi was asleep from anesthesia, Dr. Becker made small cuts in each side of the fingers. He took pieces of healthy muscle from another part of the hand and placed them in the slits. Carefully closing the wound, he applied clean bandages and a plaster splint.

Slowly, after two months of special exercises, Munandi felt his hand come back to life. He stretched out his fingers and picked up a stone. He fed himself with a spoon. Now he could work and take care of his family.

The doctor then ventured into nerve surgery, relieving the pain in hands and arms for leprosy patients who could not sleep because of the pain. A witch doctor named Vubisi was cured of his leprosy at Oicha. He became a Christian, studied the Bible and later was made a leader in the church.

Deep in the Ituri Forest around Oicha lived the pygmies. The grownups were sometimes no taller than an average man's waist. The pygmies had light copper-colored skin with tight little curls all over their heads. They were a carefree people, seldom leaving the forest. They were the Congo's gypsies, never staying long in one place, living only to eat, sleep, hunt and play.

Since Oicha's mission station had been founded with the hope of reaching the pygmies, Jim Bell and his wife had often gone into the forest to witness to these people. But so far very few pygmies ever stopped there.

"The other African tribes don't consider the pygmies human," said Dr. Becker to his wife. "They look down upon the pygmies."

He prayed, asking God for wisdom in helping the Africans understand a pygmy, was an important person in God's sight, with a soul worth saving.

Show Illustration #19

One day when the doctor had an especially long line of patients waiting in the hot sun for their medicine, he noticed a little pygmy fellow carrying his dog approach the front desk to give his name and tell his problem. Pygmies used dogs which did not bark for hunting.

All the medical students began to laugh. "The doctor isn't busy enough, so this little guy brings his sick dog to keep the doctor busy!"

"Ha-ha-ha, he thinks the *munganga* will look at a mongrel dog!"

Dr. Becker felt this just might be the answer to his prayer. When the medical assistants saw the doctor coming, they stopped making fun of the little man.

"I'll pay his fee," said the doctor. (A few pennies was the charge to register at the medical clinic for the year. This was done to give patients a feeling of having paid their way.)

"Oh, he has paid," said a helper, hiding his smile. He pointed to the three pennies on the desk. "It's just that this unimportant creature brings you a dog to treat!"

The doctor knelt and took the dog in his arms. "*Munganga*," said the little man, "I was hunting monkeys when a very angry one fell upon my dog and bit him. I am afraid he will die."

"Come into my office," said the doctor, and he let the pygmy go ahead of all the patients who were waiting. The pygmy's wife followed.

There wasn't a sound after the medical assistants stopped laughing. Dr. Becker treated the pygmy with his dog just as kindly as he treated everyone else. *Perhaps he will tell his tribe, and others will come*, thought the doctor. *At least my assistants have seen that every single person is treated equally here at Oicha.*

Although much time went by after that, few pygmies came to the hospital. "Well, then," said Dr. Becker, "if the pygmies won't come to us, we will go to the pygmies."

A missionary, Margaret Clapper, went into the rain forest some years later and searched for pygmy camps and villages. Miss Clapper became a missionary to the pygmies, hiking miles of jungle paths on foot.

Miss Clapper had 4,000 pygmy names written in a booklet she carried. One-third of them professed to receive Christ through the efforts of the Bells and Miss Clapper and at Oicha hospital where they had finally begun going when they got sick.

Oicha had become a place of miracles where God never failed to send what was needed–just in time. It was a place where a Christian doctor, nurses, missionaries and African medical assistants loved and cared for people no one else would touch. And it was a place where Christians loved pygmies enough to go into the jungle and search for them so they could hear that Jesus died for them.

Wonderful things happened almost every day at Oicha, but there was terrible trouble ahead that even the doctor could not imagine! There was an explosion coming that would shake the entire world!

Chapter 4
THE CONGO EXPLODES!

Fear ye not, stand still and see the salvation of the Lord which He will show you today.
(Exodus 14:13)

Show Illustration #20

It was a little after 5 a.m. when Dr. Becker opened his Bible one day the beginning of January 1960. He knew that by reading the Bible and praying, God would show him how to handle the problems the Oicha station and the whole mission faced. Not only was he a doctor, but he was now also the Field Director for Africa Inland Mission.

The Belgian Congo was in turmoil. Many nations of the world knew that the Congo was rich in ivory, gold, tin, copper, diamonds and rubber. Some nations wanted Congo. Many African leaders wanted Congo. And the people of the Congo wished to be free to rule themselves. Some of the would-be leaders, in their frustration to gain power, became terrorists. There was unrest everywhere, even on the mission stations. Many of the Belgian doctors fled the country. The hospital at Oicha was crowded with patients.

Dr. Becker opened his Bible to Exodus and began reading: "Fear ye not, stand still and see the salvation of the Lord which He will show you today" (Exodus 14:13). He underlined the words before continuing his devotions. Then, after praying, he began a busy day seeing patients and handling mission business.

On June 30, 1960 the Belgian Congo celebrated Independence Day from the rule of Belgium. Before and after this time, every so often, the Congo erupted in tribal wars and conflict with the government. The people had wished to be free, but they had not been prepared for freedom.

Show Illustration #21

By July all the news was alarming. Missionaries at other stations in the Congo had been threatened and harmed. Some had left the country. One morning Dr. Becker shocked his coworkers by saying, "Be ready to evacuate in one hour!"

Many things hindered their leaving, including an emergency operation and the delay of messengers bringing news. As field director, the doctor knew he was responsible for the safety of all the missionaries and their families. He also knew the presence of white people in Oicha would endanger his African friends.

The evacuation was put off until the next morning. Then Dr. Becker read again the words from Exodus, when God's people were being chased by the enemy. "Stand still!" God was ordering him. Yet how could he?

Another day passed with reports of the terrorists getting closer. Dr. Becker finally went to the church at Oicha. The building was filled with 800 Africans. They listened as he spoke, "We feel it is necessary for all missionary personnel to leave Oicha."

Show Illustration #22

Yet the words, "Stand still!" wouldn't go away. Late that afternoon, Dr. Becker heard horns honking and crowds shouting. Down the road came a shiny, black Cadillac, another car and a jeep full of soldiers. Were they terrorists? No! They were government officials from the capital.

The captain of the army and soldiers had come to protect them.

These important men paraded up to the doctor's home. Each made a long speech in French, asked Becker not to leave Oicha, and promised safety for everyone. The doctor agreed to stay.

Then the most important official made a speech to the crowd of people outside: "The hospital at Oicha is under the protection of the Belgium Government. The doctor is staying."

"*Munganga*! *Munganga*!" the crowds cheered for joy.

Dr. Becker knew the Lord had brought these officials. He heard again the words in his mind: "Stand still."

One morning the nurses discovered they had no Aspirin, very little Sulfa and no Lysol (used to sterilize equipment in the operating rooms). The supplies had been ordered long ago. Had they fallen into the hands of the terrorists?

Show Illustration #23

Dr. Becker called his coworkers together for prayer. "Our heavenly Father knows what we need before we ask," he said, "but He wants us to ask in faith and trust Him."

They worked through the morning, then stopped at noon to unpack three crates marked "Electric Light Fixtures." Dr. Becker wanted his operating room and examining rooms to be well-lit and bright. (A gasoline-powered generator provided electricity.)

Show Illustration #24

"Look at this!" The doctor held up a small box labeled "Aspirin." There were hundreds more inside. After the three crates had been emptied, they counted 50,000 Aspirin, 400,000 Sulfa pills and a big, steel drum of Lysol. There were no electric light fixtures, but Dr. Becker and the nurses weren't a bit disappointed.

Another time they had no milk for the orphans. After prayer, a truck screeched to a halt outside the hospital. The driver left 30 pounds of powdered milk by the door, jumped into his truck and drove quickly away. They never learned his name.

Show Illustration #20

The Congo's many wars continued into 1961, creeping closer and closer to Oicha. In January, Dr. Becker was reading his Bible one morning when these verses seemed to stand up on the page and wave at him:

"Hear, O Israel, ye approach this day unto battle against your enemies: let not your hearts faint, fear not, and do not tremble, neither be ye terrified because of them; for the Lord your God is He that goeth with you, to fight for you against your enemies, to save you" (Deuteronomy 20:3-4).

Faint–fear–tremble–terrified. The doctor couldn't help but wonder what the new year would bring. What would happen to make them all remember that verse? He soon found out.

That very week terrorists overthrew the Kivu Province government and planned to murder all foreigners. The Congo exploded in violence. The American Consul in Uganda warned all missionaries to leave. One hundred thirty Africa Inland Mission missionaries were alerted. Hundreds of other missionaries in northeast Congo prepared to flee. As Field Director for the Congo, 66 year old Dr. Becker knew he must set an example. This time they must go.

Show Illustration #25

Other missionaries arrived at Oicha after leaving their stations. In the dark of early morning, nine cars full of women, children and men of AIM evacuated. They headed for a secret crossing point which would put them safely in Uganda.

Driving toward Beni, they reached the border. As they began to ford the shallow river, a crowd of police and tribesmen leaped out of the tall grass and surrounded those who had not crossed the border into Uganda. The government administrator from Beni was their leader.

"Turn back to Congo!" he shouted. "My men are armed and will do whatever I tell them!"

"I think I am the one you are looking for," Dr. Becker spoke up. "I'm happy to go back to Oicha, but please allow the others to leave."

"We'll stay with you," said Mr. Andrew Uhlinger and his wife who had been missionaries for many years.

"And I'll stay, too," added young Dr. Herb Atkinson, who'd arrived only a few weeks before to assist Dr. Becker.

They returned to Oicha, while the others continued on to safety in Uganda.

Show Illustration #26

One day as Dr. Becker was busy treating patients in the hospital, he heard the strangest sound outside. Overhead there was a chugging and fluttering and clacking. People were shouting.

The patients ran outdoors and cried, "A big steel bird, *Munganga*." A military helicopter had dropped down into Oicha. Quickly the people jammed around the plane to touch it, to peer inside, to crawl under it. They smiled at the pilot.

Dr. Becker hurried over to greet him. The pilot was not smiling. "I have orders to evacuate you at once!"

The two doctors and Andrew Uhlinger shook their heads. "No, thank you."

Dr. Becker explained to the surprised pilot how he felt. "There does not seem to be any trouble here at Oicha. We are trusting God and He does not seem to be telling us to leave at this time."

The pilot stared at the obviously crazy missionaries and then left.

Dr. Becker returned to the work he loved, but one day he heard cries that started evacuations all over again. "The Simbas are coming! The Simbas are coming!" (Simba is the Swahili word for lion.)

Show Illustration #27

African nationals calling themselves Simbas disguised themselves in animal skins with claws over their hands. They leaped from trees upon their victims, killing and mutilating. At first they preyed upon simple villagers. Then the Simbas organized. Their wicked leaders gave them machine guns and bazookas and told them no bullet could hurt them.

In Oriental Province to the north, a battle between Simbas and the political party left 12,000 Congolese dead. Five of the AIM mission stations fell to the terrorists. Closer and closer they came to Oicha. In 1964 they invaded Stanleyville, only two days' travel away from Oicha.

The American Embassy in Uganda ordered all Americans to leave Congo. Dr. Becker knew the Simbas would never permit missionary work to continue. By staying at Oicha, he would make it dangerous for the national Christians.

Over the Oicha radio he broadcast a very short farewell message to all. Then he was gone. At age 70, after 35 years in the Congo, Dr. Becker and his wife were evacuated by truck to the safety of Uganda. Oicha was left without their beloved doctor. The people could hardly believe he was gone. Then Yonama, the African medical director, escaped with the medical staff and their families–200 people. Those left at Oicha could look to God alone for help.

The Simbas pounced upon Oicha, surrounding it with twenty armored cars besides big guns. The very sick patients could do nothing but crawl under the beds. Seven Christians were shot, one of them a teacher. The top names on the list for execution were Dr. Becker and Yonama.

Christians ran into the Ituri Forest. They crawled deep into the bushes and lived in hollow trees. Medical work came to a halt. The crippled leprosy patients who could not run lay on the floor in their huts listening to gunfire and the screaming.

After the Simbas wrecked all they could, they left. In Bunia, they arrested and tortured Christians. Two thousand people there were killed. But the worst fighting between Simba terrorists and government troops took place at Oicha.

Weeks later people returned to Oicha, a few at a time. Benjamina, now a strong Christian, encouraged the people and started up some of the medical work. The believers were left without Dr. Becker, but Dr. Becker's God was present in Oicha. Benjamina and the Christians knew God would help them. But they didn't know the surprise God had planned for them.

Chapter 5

RETURN TO PARADISE

*. . . Be ye steadfast, unmoveable, always abounding in the work of the Lord,
forasmuch as ye know that your labor is not in vain in the Lord.*
(1 Corinthians 15:58)

One month, two months, three, four, then five months passed. Still Dr. and Mrs. Becker waited in Uganda. They could not return yet to the Congo. What did God want them to do?

Dr. Becker was a physician. He healed people. He operated. One day the government of Uganda asked him to reopen a small, abandoned medical clinic and leprosy camp. Nyabirongo was a run-down group of buildings in the foothills of the Mountain of the Moon.

Dr. Becker accepted the challenge. He requested that Yonama and the 200 refugees from Oicha be allowed to live there and help him. One of the refugees was Melona, the hospital evangelist.

Melona had not always been an evangelist. When he was a boy, neither he nor his parents had heard of God or His Son. They worshiped evil spirits out of fear.

One day Melona's mother said to him, "Go to the river and bring back water." Melona tried to lift the big clay pot and fell down. He tried again, but fell, too weak this time to stand.

"Call the witch doctor," said his father. "Somebody has put a curse on my son."

Show Illustration #28

When the witch doctor arrived, he was decked out in bells, feathers and charms. He dug a hole and placed eight stones around the inside. Melona's father then named each stone after men of the village. The witch doctor swiftly cut off the head of a chicken and released the bird. The body ran, then staggered a few steps and fell across one of the stones.

"Imbi!" cried Melona's father. "Imbi put the curse on my son!"

Imbi heard his name and was terrified. Villagers had been killed for less than that. Men brought Imbi to the witch doctor.

"Spit on this leaf," ordered the witch doctor and Imbi obeyed. The witch doctor rubbed some of the chicken blood on the leaf and plastered it on Melona's chest, then his forehead, mumbling prayers all the while. Nothing happened.

"Don't let me die," moaned Melona. "Oh, don't let me die."

Over and over the witch doctor tried to cure Melona with the blood of the chicken. Finally, he gave up. After many days Melona's body healed itself until finally he could stand on his feet again.

A little later, a missionary visited Melona's village. Melona listened to what the missionary said: "The blood of animals cannot take away sin or heal. Only the blood of Jesus shed on Calvary's cross takes away sin." (See Hebrews 9:12-14.)

Melona knew he had sinned. He believed God loved him and sent His Son to die for his sin, so he accepted the Lord Jesus Christ as His Saviour. He had had enough of witch doctors and evil spirits. He wanted peace and love and a clean life which only a loving God could give.

Eventually Melona went to live at Oicha. There he became the hospital evangelist who spoke to patients about the Lord. When the Simbas attacked Oicha, Melona had fled with the other medical staff. Now he would be evangelist for the small clinic at Nyabirongo–until he could return to Oicha.

Melona, Dr. Becker and the others settled into Nyabirongo. When they arrived, a government official warned them: "Of course you realize you are living in a danger zone here, too." Dr. Becker just smiled. He was used to danger zones.

Some of the Wanandi Tribe high in the mountains around Nyabirongo had turned terrorist, raided the villages and fought the government soldiers. In spite of this, there were soon 300 ailing Ugandan people standing in line each day for medicine. Soon 600 a day came to the clinic. After only three months, there was room for one hundred bed patients, huts for leprosy and TB patients, an operating room and a maternity section for mothers and babies.

Show Illustration #29

One Sunday afternoon Dr. Becker, missionaries and medical staff gathered for an outdoor testimony meeting. They sat on large, grass mats under a grove of trees. Many of the 200 Oicha refugees told marvelous stories of God's protection during their escape to Uganda. Some shared how verses from Psalms had encouraged them. A few mothers told how God had strengthened them when their babies had been born during this time.

Dr. Becker looked around the group and then off into the distance where a mountain range climbed into the sky. *There is no place on earth that I would rather be than with these people*, he thought.

A week later Wanandi terrorists swarmed down the mountainside, whooping and throwing spears. Some villagers at Nyabirongo were injured. Animals were stolen. Fences were broken down. The Ugandan Army arrived as the Wanandi escaped up the hills. Their rifles cracked as they aimed into the woods.

All the next day Dr. Becker saw patients from dawn to dusk. He sent out one of the nurses into the hillside to round up the hospital patients who had jumped out of the windows and had run when they heard the terrorists attacking.

Show Illustration #30

Around midnight the doctor was glad to lie down and sleep. Knock! Knock! Thump! He opened the door cautiously.

"We have brought him here to die." A Wanandi tribesman pointed to a man lying face down on the doorstep.

Dr. Becker recognized the leader of the terrorists. He had been shot by a government bullet.

"Mary! Jewell!" Dr. Becker called his nurses and began to scrub for an operation. When the operation was over, the man was still seriously ill. Every day the nurses changed his bandages and spoke to him of God's love and of Jesus who died for him. They not only talked, but they also showed God's love by their kindness.

This leader of the terrorists, a man cruel to all of Nyabirongo, watched the nurses and Dr. Becker. He listened when the Gospel was presented. By the third day of treatment he was a changed man, no longer angry.

The government soon heard that the man they most wanted was at Nyabirongo. They drove up to claim him. Dr. Becker faced the men and said, "He is my patient and I have not discharged him from the hospital. When he is well, he may leave."

Two weeks later the soldiers returned and arrested the terrorist leader. He left by stretcher, hugging a Swahili New Testament.

It was a wonderful day in July 1965 when Dr. Becker was allowed by the government of the new Congo to return for a visit. He had started his missionary career 35 years earlier. He had learned to live in a mud but and had begun operating on a kitchen table. Now he was going to see how the hospital and medical work at Oicha had survived the Simbas.

A plane took him to Bunia. Then he drove by car to the custom house, headed by plane again to Beni on a forty minute flight over the Ituri Forest. From Beni he drove again with four other missionaries to Oicha.

Show Illustration #31

What a welcome! News spread along all the trails and roads. *"Munganga is* back! *Munganga* is back!" African medical assistants, leprosy patients, pygmies, crippled and bandaged patients, children, people of many tribes mobbed the car.

The best part of the welcome was seeing Benjamina running toward him. "Doctor! Hurry! We need you in the operating room! The patient is dying!" he shouted.

Dr. Becker joined Benjamina in the operating room. They worked quickly and the patient lived. As Dr. Becker stood in the quiet room, he listened to the rejoicing of the people outside. They were his people.

"Thank you, Lord," he said, "for bringing me back home again."

In December Dr. Becker returned to Oicha, then headed on to Nyankunde where he started a Medical Center. He continued to visit Oicha and other mission stations. In 1976 he retired at age 82 and returned to Myerstown, PA, with his wife.

He left at Nyankunde a Medical Center with seven medical doctors, a trained medical staff and six overseas nurses, a school for training African nurses and midwives, a central pharmacy, and eight outlying hospitals with 60 dependent rural clinics.

Do you remember the big decision Dr. Becker made when he was in Boyertown earning $10,000 a year? What choices did he have? (*Teacher:* He could have gone to Washington, DC, and made his fortune. He could have stayed in Boyertown where a rich man offered to build him a big, new hospital. Or, he could go to the lost, needy people of the Congo.)

Which did he do? Was it worth it? If he had made one of the other decisions, what might have happened?

Show Illustration #32

Many people will be in Heaven because of Dr. Becker's medical work and Christian life and witnessing.

Many of the world's people wait to hear the Good News for the first time. Will you ask God to use your life, if you are His child? Will you tell Him you will go wherever He wants you to go and give Him the rest of your life as Dr. Becker did?

Background for the Teacher

Belgian Congo was 1/3 the size of the United States, lying deep in the heart of Africa, slightly to the east (see back cover).

In 1484, Portuguese mariner Diego Cao sailed into the mouth of the Congo River. He found the Congo area to be well organized with six provinces ruled by governors. The Congo boasted roads, a postal system, and cowrie shell money. Law and order reigned. Until 1660, the tribe of Bakongo remained on good terms with the Portuguese. In 1665, the Portuguese annexed 1/2 million square miles of the Congo.

The notorious slave trade had always existed from ancient times. Soon other nations discovered the Congo and joined in the slave trade, aided by Africans and Arabs. Between the 15th and 16th centuries, 30 million Congolese were shipped away into slavery. In the late 1800s, Belgian adventurers discovered the Congo. Explorers and scientists followed. And missionaries.

In 1870, Dr. David Livingston discovered the highly organized Arab trade in African slaves. The outraged reports of explorers Stanley and later Cameron came to the attention of King Leopold II in Belgium. Under the guise of humanitarianism, he exploited the Congo for his own personal fortune. Although he allowed businessmen and missionaries to enter, the Congolese never forgot their hard lives under Leopold II.

In 1885, Leopold II made himself sovereign of what he named the Congo Free State, a territory of nearly a million square miles. To quiet an outraged Christian Church, he opened the medical clinics and schools to all missionaries. By 1890, the Arab slave traders were again stirring up tribal wars, as well as massacring and kidnapping blacks. Millions of dollars from Congo's rubber exports went into the pocket of Leopold II.

The world was alerted when Joseph Conrad, British sea captain on the Congo River, authored the novel *Heart of Darkness.* He described the unspeakable brutality of the Belgian overlords to the Congolese. Three million blacks died during the 15-year reign of Leopold II over the Congo riches.

In 1908, thanks to angry world opinion, Brussels Parliament obliged Leopold II to give up his personal Congo empire. The name of Belgian Congo, governed by the Belgian Government, replaced Leopold II's Congo Free State.

An educational program was begun. Congo was divided into six provinces: Leopoldville, Equator, Oriental, Kasai, Katanga and Kivu. Minimum wages replaced slave labor. The missionary-operated medical care was the best in all of Africa. Colonialism became paternalism, with civil liberties and limited freedoms, still with strict apartheid.

Air fields, seaports and railroads were expanded. However, none of this was adequate preparation for independence.

The Congo had natural wealth, producing tin, copper, uranium, gold, and diamonds.

In 1942, the socialists of the parliament of the Belgium Government insisted upon self-government for the Congo.

On June 30, 1960, the Republic of the Congo was officially announced. Because it had not been prepared for this responsibility so soon, a breakdown in government was followed by anarchy, tribal wars, looting, treachery and all kinds of violence. The Congo was a prize which many nations and black leaders wished to have for themselves.

In less than a week, four world powers met and clashed over the Congo (the United States, Russia, France and Belgium), and the cold war all but turned hot. Troops from the United Nations, sent in to restore order, faced an impossible situation. Murders, rebellions, treason, and atrocities followed. The Congo had literally exploded.

Dr. Carl K. Becker carried on his mission of mercy in healing and proclaiming the Gospel during this time.

Today, the Republic of Zaire covers 905,568 square miles with a population of 17,400,000, the third largest country in Africa. French is the official language. Zaire is considered to be Roman Catholic but there is religious freedom.

The pygmies are the oldest inhabitants of Zaire. There are still 300,000 of them in the Ituri Forest in the northeast section of the country.

The Bantu make up the majority of the population of Zaire. They migrated from the north 500 years B.C., and for 2,000 years continued to enter the Congo basin. There are 300 different tribes within the Bantu people.

At one time Zaire (then the Congo) had 400 native languages. Today, the principal ones are Kikongo, Tshiluba, Lingala, and Swahili.

Kinshasa, the capital, is a modern city, busy with traffic, full of apartment buildings and offices. Large national parks, lakes,4,000 islands, dense rain forests and snow-capped mountains sitting on the equator are all part of beautiful Zaire.

Review Questions
by Bryan Willoughby

Chapter 1

1. Why did the witch doctor leave a hex in front of Dr. Becker's hut? *(He wanted to put a curse on Dr. Becker and scare him away.)*
2. What materials were the African homes made from? *(The walls were made of mud or sun-dried brick and the roofs out of grass.)*
3. Why do you think Dr. Becker always had his prayer and Bible-reading time first thing in the morning? *(Perhaps because it prepared him for the challenges of each day or because he wanted this to be his first priority.)*
4. What did the nationals call Dr. Becker? *(The "mungunga")*
5. Why did Dr. Becker want his patients to be watched while they took their medicine. *(Some of the patients thought that pills and medicine bottles were supposed to scare away evil spirits or be used as good luck charms.)*
6. Who was the one person Kisobe cared about? *(His son Benjamina)*
7. What persuaded Kisobe to allow the mission station to be built? *(The missionaries promised to also build a school where Benjamina would be able to learn how to read.)*
8. What animal's blood did the witch doctor tell Kisobe was enough to take away sin? *(A chicken)*
9. At first Kisobe was afraid of no one. Did he stay this way throughout the story? What did he become afraid of? *(No. Evil spirits, curses, spells, and that God would strike him dead for lying.)*
10. How can we tell that Kisobe became a Christian for real the second time? *(His life was changed! He built a chapel in his village and wanted everyone to know about his new life in Christ.)*

Chapter 2

1. How old was Carl when his father died? *(Eleven)*
2. What did Carl's pastor tell him about making a personal decision for Christ? *(He told Carl that just having Christian parents didn't make him one. He needed to confess his own sins and believe that Jesus died for him.)*
3. Why did the African Inland Mission need missionary doctors? *(Missionary doctors cared for the people's physical needs> This let the people know that the missionary preachers and teachers cared about more than just their spiritual needs.)*
4. On a grass plot behind his house Carl made a deal with God. What did he ask God to do for him? What did he offer God in return? *(He asked God to help him become a doctor. He promised to be a missionary if God called him.)*
5. Why did Carl leave Ursinus College early? *(He needed to work to support his mother.)*
6. A month before graduation, Carl made a special request to God. What did he ask for and how did God answer his prayer? *(He asked God for a new suit for graduation. In one week he received the money he needed in gifts from friends.)*
7. What kept Carl from going to Africa right after his mandatory year at Hahnemann's hospital? *(He believed that the Bible taught that his first duty was to provide for his mother.)*
8. Why do you think Carl was willing to leave his mother several years later? *(He had earned enough money to provide for her for many years.)*
9. How old was Dr. Becker when he knew for sure that God wanted him to become a missionary? *(Thirty-five)*
10. If you had been one of Dr. Becker's patients in Boyertown would you have begged him to stay? *(Yes, because he was*

a good doctor and friend. No, so that the people in Africa who have no doctor would finally have a good one.)

Chapter 3

1. What group of people were the missionaries especially hoping to reach? *(The Pygmies)*
2. Why did Dr. Becker want to train assistants? *(Dr. Becker knew he would be able to treat more patients and give more of his attention to the serious cases.)*
3. What did Dr. Becker do to make the unwilling medical student change his mind about giving blood to Lazaro? *(He offered to give his own blood.)*
4. Why was the medical student so shocked when Dr. Becker offered to give his own blood to Lazaro? *(Because Dr. Becker was willing to give his blood to someone from another race.)*
5. Dr. Becker treated everyone with kindness, even the people nobody else cared about. Can you think of any people like that to whom Jesus showed kindness? *(The Canaanite woman in Matthew 15; the little children and blind Bartimaeus in Mark 10; the sinful woman in Luke 7; Zacchaeus in Luke 19; the Samaritan Woman in John 4)*
6. What is leprosy? *(A disease where patches of skin lose their color and ability to feel. Deformities and disabilities can result from complications.)*
7. What was Vubisi's job before he became a Christian and leader in the church? *(He was a witch doctor.)*
8. Why do you think the other African tribes didn't consider the pygmies human? *(Their small size and copper colored skin; because they stayed in the forest)*
9. What were the two reasons why Dr. Becker gave the pygmy with the dog special treatment? *(He hoped that the pygmy would tell his tribe and others would come to Oicha. He also wanted to teach his assistants to treat everyone equally.)*
10. What did the missionaries do when they realized that the pygmies were not coming to Oicha? *(They [specifically Margaret Clapper] went into the rainforest to find them!)*

Chapter 4

1. Why did different nations and African leaders want to rule the Congo? *(They wanted the valuable ivory, gold, tin, copper, diamonds and rubber found there.)*
2. Through what book of the Bible did God tell Dr. Becker to "Stand still!" Can you tell me which Bible story these words are from? *(Exodus 14:13; Parting of the Red Sea)*
3. Who arrived before the missionaries could evacuated Oicha? *(Belgium government officials, the captain of the army and soldiers)*
4. Do you think Dr. Becker was surprised to find the needed medical supplies in the boxes marked "Electric Light Fixtures?" Do you think he was surprised that God provided these things? *(Yes! Perhaps not, because God had always met his needs.)*

5. What did the terrorists who overthrew the Kivu Province plan to do to all foreigners? *(Murder them)*
6. How many missionaries offered to stay with Dr. Becker when he was forced to turn back from crossing the border into Uganda? *(Three: Mr. Andrew Uhlinger and his wife, and Dr. Herb Atkinson.)*
7. Why did Dr. Becker and the other missionaries refuse a helicopter ride to safety when they had earlier tried to leave the country on their own? *(They were trusting and waiting for God who did not seem to be telling them to leave yet.)*
8. Who were the Simbas? *(A destructive group of African terrorists who dressed like wild animals.)*
9. Why did Dr. Becker finally leave the Congo? *(The American Embassy ordered all Americans to leave. He knew the Simbas would not allow missionary work. His staying would make it more dangerous for national Christians.)*
10. Who started up the medical work and encouraged the people after Oicha had been devastated by the Simbas? *(Benjamina)*

Chapter 5

1. What did Dr. Becker do while he was waiting to see if he would be allowed to return to the Congo? *(He re-opened an abandoned medical clinic and leprosy camp in Nyabirongo, Uganda.)*
2. How did the witch doctor try to heal Meloma? *(While mumbling prayers, he mixed chicken blood and saliva on a leaf, then plastered the leaf to Meloma's chest and forehead.)*
3. What did Meloma do to become a Christian? *(He admitted that he was a sinner and then he believed and accepted Jesus who had died for his sins.)*
4. What was Dr. Becker and the nurses' attitude toward the injured terrorist leader? *(They lovingly cared for his body and spirit, just like any other patient.)*
5. What was Dr. Becker's favorite part of his return to the Congo? *(Helping Benjamina save a patient's life.)*
6. How old was Dr. Becker when he retired? *(82)*
7. What words would you use to describe Dr. Becker? *(Faithful, dedicated, wise, obedient, kind)*
8. What do you think was the most challenging time in Dr. Becker's life? *(Perhaps leaving the Congo, or first coming to the Congo, or when his father died.)*
9. In what ways did God communicate with Dr. Becker in this story? *(Through the Holy Spirit speaking to his heart, through the Bible, through other Christians [his pastor, Sunday school teacher, and wife].)*
10. During the Sunday afternoon testimony meeting Dr. Becker looked off into the distance and thought to himself, *There is no place on earth I would rather be.* Why do you think Dr. Becker felt this way? *(Because of his love for the people and because of his satisfaction in being where God wanted him to be.)*

www.ingramcontent.com/pod-product-compliance
Lightning Source LLC
Chambersburg PA
CBHW061057090426
42742CB00002B/70